MW01173776

Just Thinking Out Loud

...In a Book

By: Liphe's Place

Acknowledgment
To The Most High for
everything is possible with
faith the size of a mustard
seed
My parents, Sisters, Children
and Grands
Good friends still by my side
and those who left a long time
ago

Dedication to the lessons
learned to keep growing into
the BEing I see in front of Me

Breathe

Think out Loud

The most hurtful is
the one you least
expect

Just imagine spilling all of your
secrets for the One you trusted
to spill your secrets
everywhere...

Let Go

Choose You

Most folk are slower than you
think
Don't get upset
Be Happy
Be glad you had sense to notice
where there is none

Look in your Mirror
Look to see you to see your own
view

You really have to move from
Sadness
-The Energy
-The People
-The Place
Anything
Just because it will make you sad
about everything

Always Choose You

Sadly
Most are not mentally the same
age as their birth year

Spiteful folk will destroy
themselves in hopes it will
destroy you, too

Inhale
to
Exhale
There is goodness in
breathing for you

Live life for You

Not all are as mentally
strong as You

Breathe

Never let anyone disrupt your
life just because they have no
life

Gotta let folks water themselves

Bitterness is a disease
Be sure to stay 6ft away

Remove your Self from People,
Places & Things
no longer of value to you

Take a Nap

The mirror is your friend

You'll piss people off just for wanting to do something new for You

Insecure folk will avoid you in hopes you'll feel insecure, too

You'll be surprised how many
folks wished you didn't learn
as much as you have been

Most of the people around you
are unplugged just to stay in
the Matrix out of
comfortability

Most in powerful positions use
manipulation to keep you in one
spot

Not all are as loyal to you
as you are to them

Most are used to playing victim and will do everything to make you out to be the victimizer

Most folk offer you crumbs
then get mad that you have
cakes in the oven

It's the manipulator trying to manipulate you into believing that it was You doing the manipulating

How you keep it moving is knowing
folks will do some shiddd and not
giving a fawkkk what is said...

Most folk are used to distorting
their own view of themselves...
Most hope you see yourself the
same way, too

Trust your Gut

Remember to put on the
clothing for success

Sadly, most folk think love is
fawking someone to both fawking
each other over in the name of
"Love"
Keep it Moving

Some folk want you to be
stepford minded to
everything around you
Reality is hard on most folk

You have to pay mind to the
theaters you walk into

Most are stages set up for
you to walk on

Most are set up to make it
look like you are part of the
Cast & Crew

Who is Directing You?

Breathe

Are you the Director
or
A part of the Crew
...when it comes to the life you
live for You...
Are you the Director of...
Your happiness...
Your peace
Joy
Laughter
...Your smile
Be sure you are the Director
for all You do for You

There's joy in loving on yourself
for as long as you want to...
How often are you by yourself...
How often are you in the quiet by
Yourself...

Ground Yourself

Speak goodness to yourself in front of every mirror

There's love, curiosity,
knowledge and new experiences
when you're around others that
want love, fulfills their
curiosty, knowledge is sought
after and new experiences lead
to even more new experiences
as One

Grow a plant or two
Learn about more than a few
Grow more than you want to
You'll grow more than the
plants around You

Blessings
Truth is
Money ain't a thang
Thrifted and donated goods carry
named brands, too

Never question the thirst around
You
Most are used to empty cups
filled with air

Some folk get upset when you offer packs of peen to suck on instead of your energy

Some folk just need your
energy to feel alive

You have to come to terms with
your own truth and accept it

Not all have majik just as not all
know how to spell

Can't drink from empty cups...
Most expect you to get thirsty
waiting for them to pour you some
water

The people around you should be
living a life of their own, too

Folks will always find someone else
to do what they don't want to do
Most know what they want to do is
wrong
Most are just hoping you're just
that slow to do what they don't
want to do

Most folk will believe the one with the phony tears and big tits before the One that looks like a bum never asking anyone for anything

Sometimes the mask hides the
constant tears
No one knows what's behind
anyone's mask
Be You
Mask on or off

Most folk will not see you for
you
It's no matter as long as you see
You for You

Be your own friend, best friend & confidant

Breathe

Careful of those who say they
dream of someone like you as most
will fawkk you right out of your
own dreams

Some folk will come back
around dressed up to "help"
you with your success to only
destroy what you've succeeded
dressed up in a suit

Crazy thing is that we are all One with One another yet most are not even One with themselves... The cycle continues...

Never be surprised as to
who comes back around
hoping for a plate of food

The path is straight & Narrow
The body can do amazing things
Contortionists, anyone?
Yoga, Pilates, Stretch
The Mind is the strength in what
the body can do
Challenege you

Can't be at War with Your
Self and those around you, too

Who's Sins are you paying for?

Will you save every drowning folk
when you can barely swim your
SELF

Gotta pay mind to those who are
easily influenced by money,
power & connections as most are
not even connected to
The Most High

Some folk are obsessed
with power to move people
around yet is easily angered
when moved by their
obsessive behavior...

Choose You

It is really is about being
considerate in places
where you were never
considered

Plant yourself into the pot
of fertile soil and grow into
as many possibilities as
possible....

You are going to outgrow a lot of
people around you
Keep Growing Anyway

Most just want you to do all the
heavy lifting

Its only a problem when you switch around how you play every game played on you

Most folk think you need their friendship when you never needed a friend who is not even a friend to you

Everyone that comes around you
is a visitor to your court
Most want to rent space while
others live in spaces never meant
for long stays...

You can swim deeper than those
around you

Breathe

Most will return with old chairs
hoping for a seat

The cycle continues...

Never chase mirrors
Chase Your Self

You are Love

There's nothing and no one
more important than You

Most folk just want you to swallow their misery as if it's your last meal...

Choose You

Be You

Healing is a journey
Take your time in getting to know
you all over again

Don't believe everything you see
or hear as most are just set up or
appearances only

Never settle for just the appetizers when there is plenty of ingredients all around you to make your own meals

Keep the pace
Turtles pace
Take your time
Enjoy the scenary

Breathe

Enjoy You
Enjoy you for You
Enjoy you Over All

The choice has always been
yours
Always choose You

Love

Keep Writing Your Story

Made in the USA
Columbia, SC
08 January 2024

29368337R00059